Network Income

"How to Successfully Network to build strong business relationships and create Lifelong Income"

By John D'Acunto

Copyright © 2018 by John D'Acunto

All rights reserved. No part of this publication may be reproduced, distributed, or transmitted in any form or by any means, including photocopying, recording, or other electronic or mechanical methods, without the prior written permission of the publisher, except in the case of brief quotations embodied in critical reviews and certain other non-commercial uses permitted by copyright law. For permission requests, write to the publisher, addressed "Attention: Permissions Coordinator," at the address below.

For more information or to contact the author, please visit:

www.JohnDAcunto.com

Contents

Intro: What is Business Networking 4

Why Do We Network 13

    Referrals 13

    Speaking engagements 14

    Advice and Education 16

    Credibility 18

    Confidence 21

    Responsible 22

    Friendships 23

Types of Networking 27

    Social networking 30

    Strategic Networking 39

    Structured Networking 49

Where Do We Network 61

    Chamber of Commerce 61

    Service Organizations 65

    Ethnic groups. 65

    Other service organizations are Kiwanis and Rotary clubs. 67

    Recreational Clubs. 68

    Other Places to Network 72

    Social on-line Networking 74

Preparing to Network 80
    Clothing. 83
    Business Cards. 88
    Prepare your questions. 91
    Elevator Speech 92
Get Comfortable Networking 96
    Food and Drink 98
    Marketing Materials, Swag 101
    Identify 104
    Be Valuable 105
    Follow Up 107
Joining a Structured Networking Group 110
Becoming successful in a Structured Leads Organization. 114
Conclusion 119
About the Author 123

Intro: What is Business Networking

Business Networking can be as complex or as simple as you want. Networking is a socioeconomic business activity by which businesspeople and entrepreneurs meet to form business relationships and to recognize, create, or act upon business opportunities, share information and seek potential partners for ventures.

That should say enough, but it doesn't.

Business networking is leveraging your business and personal connections to bring you a regular supply of new business. The concept sounds simple, but don't let that fool you. Networking involves relationship building, which is complex and takes time to cultivate.

Networking is a conscious thought process where you collect information, and give information. You have an objective of what you want to do, and what you want to get out of the conversation at the time. It is intentional and calculated. The objective might be to get more business or, how to utilize others you meet for your own referral sources. Business networking is much more than showing up at networking functions, shaking a lot of hands and collecting a bunch of cards.

Most people don't like having business cards pushed upon them.

There's a finesse to working a room, and you have control over who you meet.

What do you think networking is about? Take a moment, think back and say to yourself.... "When was I consciously networking"? "What questions did I ask"? "What information did I learn"? What was useful in the conversation, and how did it feel? "Was I comfortable in my own skin"? "Is the party I am speaking with interesting"? Is that party interested in hearing about me?

Networking involves business owners and professionals meeting and forming relationships with like-minded individuals. As relationships materialize, familiarity and trust grow. Networking is telecommunicating whether it is, online or face to face. Our millennials today are Facebooking, Snapchatting, Tweeting. Congregating without congregating. Having conversations without looking up to see if anyone is even in the room. Yes, they may be networking alright. But how have they been connecting at this moment? What information is being translated for the time spent?

When we talk about networking, we are not just looking at direct referrals from people we are in contact with personally. There is a bigger picture here, because those that directly refer us clients are the catalyst for future referrals. You see when I look at networking in my sphere of influence, I am also expecting, that who I help, will also become an additional referral source.

For example, as a Mortgage Loan Originator, someone refers me to a relative, I do their mortgage loan, and it's possible they refer me to their boss. In turn, their family member. From there, a friend looking for a mortgage, and their friend, and their friend. But when I track back how much business I did from that one relationship, the dynamics of using good networking skills becomes even more important.

I remember when a Doctor friend of mine referred one of his patients to me. I worked diligently to find a suitable loan program for her. It must've taken five different wholesale banks before I came up with an affordable option. The client was so happy she referred me to her Aunt who was looking to get financed on a home she was interested in. She bragged about how I spent so much time helping her, that her Aunt was already sold on using me. Even if something didn't work out exactly as planned, it didn't matter because she was so hyped up from what her niece told her about me, the expectation was that I cared, and was helpful. The niece was not only happy with me, but she was so happy with her doctor for referring me, that she referred more patients to him. That is where the net, of networking starts to materialize. We never know where our next deal is coming from, so when we build those strong relationships, business flows a little more constant.

Take a moment, grab a pen and paper while I wait..... Now ask yourself, and write down, where did I last use the skill of networking? Where were you? How did the conversation start? What did I learn from it?

Networking is a natural behavior that we don't always realize we're doing. We can network everywhere. But to make it useful, we must be in the moment, for some it comes easily, for others it is a skill that's learned.

Picture this, you're in the supermarket looking at some produce to choose. There's a woman next to you in a business suit looking at some fruit. Because you're also a business person you feel comfortable commenting on whether she knows anything about picking sweet cantaloupe. Although she's not experienced in picking the cantaloupe it really doesn't matter, A conversation might start with, "hey I like your suit". She thanks you for the compliment and you comment, "Lawyer, Financial Advisor"? "No, I'm a banker with ABC Bank". Now, your both sharing information. The sharing of this information can lead to much more, it's just a matter of how far you want to go in the conversation.

Yes, your networking. You may be on your way to building a relationship that could last for years to come, and it all started with fruit.

Let me ask, can you think of a few people you know now, that you may have met in a comparable situation. Pick three business professionals in your world, where did you meet them? How long have you've known each other? Maybe you were waiting for a table at a restaurant and struck up a simple conversation to pass the time. That's how it all begins. Indulging in conversation.

How about this, when you're at a restaurant and must wait for a table. Instead of leaving your name to be called, you leave the name of your business. "MDK Financial Group, table of two". I would call that a form of networking. Networking is getting your name out there.

What about sitting in the service lounge of a car dealership. How many conversations have you stirred up then?

Think about it. How many people do you know? How many of these people truly understand what you do? Have you struck up a conversation with someone, then found you could use their service or product? You take their card, and many times they ask what do you do for a living. So, you say something like "I help families build financial security by designing a wealth strategy for their future".

Do you know any longtime friends, that your relationship started out just this way?

Conversing anytime, can basically be networking.

My neighbor down the block has a leaf blower I can borrow. Let me use my neighborhood network.

Discussing the affairs of the community can also lead to business. Don't be ashamed to start a conversation anywhere.

If you were a Realtor, and I told you the person standing next to you is looking for a Realtor to find him a One-million- dollar home, you would more than likely strike up a conversation.
The thing is, you wouldn't know they were looking, unless you opened a dialog with him or her.

Some people get frustrated with networking. It's work. You're always ON. Striking up a conversation. Strategizing your next question. Working to keep the conversation going.

It's a Practice, like a Lawyer practicing law, you're practicing, and always learning. Always inventing new ways, to engage.

It really is a skill to practice. We are always learning new ways to gather and exchange ideas. The education in how to present yourself and how to receive others.

How about the long-term friend you know from business? You didn't always know each other. Where did you meet? Could it have been at a networking event? Maybe someone you cold called on, or someone that approached you, referred by a friend or associate.

Picture you're standing in a room full of people, in a conversation with someone, and a friend of yours walks over, You, would most likely extend an introduction to everyone you're standing with. You might even suggest your friend has some business service or product of value to the person you're speaking with. Or maybe this new-found acquaintance has something your friend is, in need of? That's just another form of networking. The Net gets larger and larger as time goes by. However, it doesn't get that way without putting in the effort.

I've been involved with a large business leads group for over 20 years. I have met countless numbers of people through this one organization.

Sometimes when I'm standing around talking with some of the members, I think about how long I've known them. I ask myself, "Wait, how long do I know you"? "where did we first meet"? It amazes me on how our relationship grew overtime and we never even realize where it all began. The limitless referrals and contacts exchanged through the years is heartfelt and natural. The good times, and the solace. Frank Sinatra sang *"strangers in the night"*. I think of networking as, "strangers in the right". You are strangers until you meet and engage.

Just meeting people is not enough. Charming them and being engaged, amounts to the exchange of information, which can lead to an enormous amount of business through the art of networking.

We put a lot of effort into building these contacts. Now let's talk about why.

In this book, we touch on the benefits and dynamics of Face to Face networking, and how it can help you, **grow** your business.

Why Do We Network

Business Networking is a valuable way to expand your knowledge, learn from the success of others, get new clients and tell others about your occupation. It's a way to build sustainable business for the future.

Here are some of the Whys of networking:

Referrals

Quality referrals are the number one reason why business owners participate in networking activities and join networking groups. Referrals from networking tend to be of higher quality. They are usually pre-qualified. Someone used your service or product and wants to tell someone else how happy they are with you. They're already selling You.

Referrals are practically pre-sold clients. You're already being recommended by someone that the caller trusts in some way, and the opportunities are endless.

When you have a group of business owners you're networking with, not only are you looking at good solid referrals, but also opportunities. Opportunities in partnerships or joint ventures.

For example, if you're a Financial Advisor, will some sort of *legal product,* or system be a new venture you can incorporate into your own business for an additional income source, and in turn, help your clients. There are many opportunities out there when we look hard enough, and our referral source can be our next venture partner.

Speaking engagements

You can promote to your referral sources that you're willing to step in at their service club or trade club and speak on a subject of their interest. Speaking to a room of people can turn into a wealth of referrals. So, from one referral source you get many more. You're telling the masses about, who you are and how you can help them.

Is there an opportunity to pair up with a business buddy and present in partnership to an attentive audience on how you both can work together to service the needs of others?

There are selling and buying opportunities everywhere when referral sources exist. You discover fresh ideas from them.

Just think, what are your referral sources doing that works for them, and how can you emulate their strategies for your gain?

Your referral sources want to refer you to others. It makes them feel good about themselves, they feel needed.

They could be that "A" personality enjoying the high energy they get from introducing new contacts to each other, and being recognized for it.

"It's not who you know, it's who knows you". Sure, you can name drop, (and by the way nobody likes that). but when you get others talking about you, then it's, **_who knows you time_**.

What does this sound like? "Hey it's Mike". Mike's here". "You know Mike right"? "No, well let me introduce you".

That's**, _Who, knows you._ _A_**nd it's a good place to be. You're the Networking King. Even if you don't think so, others do.

With networking, you're building a firm source of connections. These connections will be calling on you, just as you will be calling on them. The opportunities can open doors to highly influential people that you may not have been able to connect with by merely cold calling. Influential people know other influential people, that know, more influential people.

Personal introductions are key. The connections are not only direct, they can be indirect. Who you are talking to will probably have a network of individuals themselves.

When I look back on my clientele', I can go deep into 20 or 30 clients and track back where one referral generated a pool of income, due to the many referring me.

These are all opportunities to increase your network. You are exponentially building your sphere of influence, and it is, word of mouth.

Advice and Education

Having like-minded business owners to talk to gives you the opportunity to brainstorm and pass along ideas. Brainstorming encourages people to come up with thoughts and ideas that can, at first, seem a little crazy, but helps to free up the mind and experience other people's frame of reference.

Brainstorming can be crafted into original and creative solutions to solve problems and increase opportunities. Many times, helping to jolt you out of your normal way of thinking. Brainstorming is not criticizing, but carries a positive influence for creation of ideas. This is the time to explore solutions.

Fellow business professionals can help you navigate through business decisions and even help with work-life balance. Through networking you can learn how other business owners in your industry survive and thrive.

Here is something to consider: List the challenges you have, and think about who you currently know that may be going through the same trials.

Do you think they would want your feedback?

I'm sure they will.

Any business owner, salesperson, credited professional, etc. that is already, or wants to be successful, relies on the input of others. We educate each other if we take off the blinders and are receptive to other experiences. We are learning and creating. Networking is a perfect way to tap into the experts in your field, so they can help mentor you along.

Education is a key to learning. Ask the business professionals you are networking with now. What books are they reading? How have those books helped them? What accredited courses are helping them progress in their careers? They may have courses due to their professional licensing requirements or just something they came across that seemed helpful. What they learned can be helpful to you as well, in one way or another.

With who, will they share their valuable information? It's with the people they trust and already have relationships. Building those networks of education and mentoring is extremely valuable.

Credibility

The quality of being believed or accepted as true, real, honest.

Credibility is a judgment that the audience makes about how believable the communicator is. And it's important because people often choose to respond to a persuasive message based not on the content but on their perception of the communicator. Whether it's credibility in your industry or just in your community, credibility in networking can help build a higher profile for yourself. Getting your name out there and building a stellar reputation is a reflection on the people referring business to you.

When I'm referring clients to my trusted business associates, my integrity is on the line. How will they remember me? Did I do the right thing?

Sometimes it's just a gut feeling. How comfortable am I, to refer someone?

Knowing the personality and the demeanor of both parties is important. I ask myself, have I done my best to put these two together? Have I shown my true colors to assist, or have I just said to use this person because I wanted to be a casual hero?

Getting people to know they can count on you, will undoubtedly get you more quality business leads since you will be, the one people remember.

You're the "Go to Person". Your reputation precedes you. <u>Who knows you</u> is what it's about?

What are others saying about you?

We call on people we trust, and we refer to people we trust. You will be called upon more often because others depend on you.

I have had more people call on me, because someone I knew was trusted by the individual that knew me.

You'll hear, comments like, "My good friend says you're the one I can depend on. If my buddy says you're the one, then I trust his/her judgement". Those are powerful referrals.

It's what everyone in business wants to hear. What do you remember more, how bad someone was, or how good someone was?

Seems like Bad makes the news more, and usually what people remember. Building credibility takes time.

Picture a child with building blocks. Carefully stacking, and stacking, Fully, focused on each step, Concentrating on every move. How quickly their little brother can come in the room and knock them down. That's your reputation. Build it, nurture it, and protect it.

Don't burn bridges. Talk only good of others. Rumors get started way too easy. How many times do you hear someone talking ill of someone? If they're talking bad about them, then they're probably talking bad about you at some point. Don't be that person.

On that note, remember to always find the good in everyone you meet. Find one thing you like about them. In hopes, the same will happen for you.

Confidence

Networking builds confidence.

It's the state of feeling certain about the truth of something. The feeling of self-assurance arising from one's appreciation of one's abilities or qualities.

Confidence should never be conceitful, but only appreciated. Why is confidence so important in networking? The more confident you feel, the more you feel comfortable to attend events and mingle with the crowd. The more you mingle with the crowd, the more versed you become in conversation and engagement. The more versed you become in conversation and engagement, the more confident you are in being out there, and so on, and so on.

When you're out at business mixers, networking, shoulder to shoulder with your peers, and in public, the more confident you feel.

The more you network, the more people expect to see you at networking events or business community luncheons.

These events are so important, it's your marketing time. It's a circle of events in a way. People recognize you when you walk in the room. These are the ones that extend an introduction to whoever they are engaged with, instead of you always worrying about making the first move. You tend to hang around with more successful people as that confidence builds. Those successful individuals hang around with other successful individuals.

Becoming a powerful conversationalist allows you to command a dialog and take it where you want it to go.

This takes practice, and indulging in networking helps to build the confidence you need. You become confident in the power of conversation. But remember in the words of Peter Parker's grandfather in Spiderman, "with great power comes great responsibility". So, keep in mind, as you become popular and great in networking, your peers will be counting on you. Now you become responsible for your reputation and the reputation of others.

Responsible

As referenced previously, networking helps you, help others. You become the "go to person". Your business associates, friends and family members start to realize that you have a network of business professionals, and they call on you when they need a reference.

Again, it's your reputation, and the reputation of others that put you and them in the marketplace.

Assisting other business people in your community has a good feeling attached to it as well, and the more responsible you can be for their success, the more you are noticed by the public. This helps them keep you, in the forefront of their minds.

Friendships

Powerful friendships develop from years of networking. You just never know what relationships come out of successful networking. We can lose track of how many friendships we formed over time.

I have lost touch with quite a few business friends I have met from networking. Some I haven't seen for a few years and, out of the blue they appear back in my life. A circle of friendships rotating over time.

A thought, a post on social media, or a happened chance running into someone at a grocery store or business mixer, reconnects us.

As briefly just explained, networking through Face to Face introductions can provide numerous benefits.

What is the best way to secure business? Word of Mouth. What happens to a restaurant when patrons talk about how great the food is, the ambiance, the service. It goes from mouth to mouth, ear to ear.

Many people trust what their friends, family and associates say. The most obvious benefit is, increase in business. The referrals you get from networking are usually high quality and pre-qualified.

We network to build strong long-lasting relationships. Business networking helps with credibility.

Countless times my friends, and clients will call on me when they need a referral for a service or product they're in need of, why? Because they know I have trusted professionals that I have built relationships with over time.

Having these people trust who I recommend adds to my credibility and makes me a dependable resource.

Having a strong network of business owners empowers me to be a valuable resource.

The more people that connect with you for your recommendation, the more opportunities it is to earn more business.

Our happy clients are our biggest resource of new business. Depend on them as a core marketing arm.

Current and previous clients you continually connect with usually trust what, or who you recommend. They probably wouldn't be your customers if they didn't. The benefits are enormous.

For example, I was referred a client to help find financing for their prospective new home. They met me at my office. As we sat down to complete a loan application, I noticed that the designated wage earner in the family did not have any Life or disability Insurance. As I questioned my new client as to what would happen to his family if something in the way of an accident happened to him, whether he was hurt and couldn't work or worse, died suddenly, how would his family survive financially?

It's not the most enjoyable conversation, but It was something he hadn't thought of before. Fortunately, I had an Insurance Agent I trusted and relied on to help go over the products and services that could keep my client's family secure in the event of a catastrophic event.

Simply put, there was a need I was able to fill due to the trusted people I network with. He was new in town and had no contacts locally. At the same time, I referred him to my home & auto agent to make sure his home was covered by insurance, the Handyman I knew, for any simple repairs he needed done in the home, and countless others that I networked with. My client kept talking about how amazing it was that I could direct him to any business professional he needed. He also referred me a lot of clients as he gained his footing in the community.

This was not a flash in the pan. This scenario happens many times because I have the resources in my network. Networking is also a way of learning. Learning about other businesses. Good networking skills can help you understand how other businesses work and the challenges they have. What makes these business owners tick? How do they operate and what pushes their buttons? Knowing how others do things can help get your foot in the door.

You network to collaborate. You don't need to be an expert, but when you understand someone else's business a little more, you can utilize your own resources to help them find solutions to their business challenges.

How do they do business? Let me also ask, How, do their values compare to yours? What type of clients are they looking for? How can you, help them?

You can ask them, are you looking for more business? What type of clients are you looking for?

Types of Networking

We'll discuss here, three specific types of networking.

We network in various situations, and making use of that time is important. The **old paradigm**: show up, hand out business cards. Collect as many as you can, talk about how great you are.

Just cause you show up doesn't mean you're in the moment. Just showing up doesn't automatically put money in your pocket. Pushing your business card into someone's hand is not the way of doing business. It does not make the best, "First Impression".

How many times have you attended an event, and as you first walk in the door someone is standing right at the entrance forcing their business card on you? They're expecting that you're going to read it and magically be drawn to their service or product. Think back, has this happened to you, and where is that business card now? Many years ago, I attended a networking event where a gentleman asked me for my business card. Didn't even introduce himself first, and after I handed it to him, he mentioned how I wasn't quick enough handing it to him. He tried to explain how I should be locked and loaded, quick on the draw to hand my business card to him. This sounded crazy to me. Where's the finesse. I agree that you want to have your business cards within easy reach, but he made it sound like a competition, **The old paradigm,**

I thanked him for the advice and don't believe I ever saw him again.

As quickly as you want to talk about yourself, don't.
The old paradigm is how can I impress you with my services as quickly as I can, so I can move on to the next attendee. Yes, I'm great. I guess you are too. But let me tell you about me.
No, let's build a relationship, that's where the business is.

New paradigm: Networking involves building quality relationships one person at a time. Meeting who you want, and getting to know some important things about them in a matter of minutes. Who are you, what do you do, and, *how can I help you*, is a powerful impression to make. Caring about others. Being truly interested in what they do. Be Authentic, remember that word. Being yourself and being true to the ones you engage with, is how relationships flourish.

Just cause we're networking in a crowded setting doesn't mean we can get to everyone. But allocating a certain amount of time to who we want to meet, helps us discover quality connections. Sure, you won't hit the masses, but you will discover the quality people. Quality people are the ones with knowledge about their business, and industry. They are the ones that know people you want to know. They are the ones that make connections and are quick to introduce you. They enjoy stimulating conversation. You are Quality, you are the one that can help bridge relationships.

Help to make everyone you meet feel special. One person at a time. Relationships take time and effort.

With all the technology of not meeting people in person, this is the time that when we do meet in person, we want to make it count. Select conversation and awareness helps you discover what sparks people's interest.

With many people so self-absorbed, it's important to make them feel special. We all do it. We get caught up in talking about ourselves.

I catch myself doing the same thing. When I do, I take a step back and put myself in check. The next networking event you attend, as you're in the conversation, take a step back while listening and be aware of your engagement, you may surprise yourself.

Don't worry, make it about them and you'll make a new friend. Engage, engage, engage when networking. Getting to know people in different settings and why they're there is what it's about.

Many times, I'll choose my conversation to meet my needs by asking questions. People like to explain their business, let them talk. Practice asking questions. Depending on the type of event, you may want to prepare how you'll show up. We'll discuss Preparation later.

Our next dialogue will cover three essential types of networking:

Social Networking, Strategic Networking and Structured Networking.

Social networking

Social Networking involves some informality and may be inconsistent in the way the gatherings are structured and attended. This type of networking includes informal or formal networking events. Not to say there is no agenda, but usually informal in the sense of attendance, or total commitment of the attendees. You may, or may not see the same people over and over. It's the type of event where showing up on time, or after the scheduled time to attend, is open to your own discretion. People that attend do so, on how they feel that day.

Social networking can yield bridges of influence, but there's an element of luck because of the lack of consistency.

Many come to a meeting or two, don't get business so they don't return. They don't understand that, effort and continued exposure takes time and energy.

I remember talking to a local business owner who said to me after just once attending a community Chamber of Commerce business function; "yea, I was at a chamber mixer once, but I didn't get any business from it". I tried to explain that he should schedule their monthly mixers into his calendar and make every effort to attend each month for at least one year. I told him even if he missed a month or two after attending twelve meetings, the consistent ones that always show up will feel you're always there anyway. you're accountable, and that can add to your credibility.

With Social networking, rather than a formal agenda, attendees stand around and meet and greet more informally, each having their own specific agenda.

These events may be too informal to provide real quality business.

When I first moved to Las Vegas, I wanted a place to meet people, and began with the local Chamber of Commerce.

Nothing formal, just a way of learning who was in the community that I could network with. I wasn't looking for commitment, I was looking to test the waters. Who's here, what do they do, how do they feel about life and business, how does the community work for them. I wanted business, with a social atmosphere so I could feel comfortable first, and then take steps to serious networking.

You see, way back, when I was in my 20s, I started selling Real Estate in my home town of Brooklyn NY, I didn't realize how important networking was. My Broker belonged to a Rotary organization and encouraged me to meet with them, said I had to get to meet more people and build relationships like he had. I was young, I didn't know better. Now I look back and realize all the business I may have missed out on. Now I realize that there are multiple avenues of networking that can be beneficial. Here is where the social aspect comes in.

Social Networking, involves local business mixers, where they usually have many trades people in the same industry showing up, so you are in competition with other local businesses in your field. Natural networkers, like Realtors, Financial Professionals and Life Insurance agents just to name a few, are usually abundant.

Depending on how you look at it, this can be a conflict, or an opportunity to show why you are unique. I often found out a lot of information from people in my own industry. I didn't look at it as competition, but an excellent way to improve what I do, and how I handle my clients, compared to how others handle theirs.

I remember talking with another mortgage lender at a social networking mixer, he kept commenting on some of his borrower clients. Making fun of what they didn't know about mortgages. I thought to myself, why would you make fun of people that are putting money in your pocket, helping you support your family. I was new in the mortgage business, but I thought to myself, I'll never put down my customers or talk ill of them especially in public, especially to a stranger. That is one important thing I learned while out networking, and it has stuck with me forever.

It's always a learning experience, always an opportunity.

Attendees at networking events are like-minded individuals. They are there for similar reasons looking to make connections and develop new relationships.

What I hoped for, materialized, and satisfied me for the meanwhile. I met community professionals that were the stepping stone of my networking voyage.

Here are some more identifiers to Social Networking.

Social networking can either be at a private venue or public venue. Some organizers plan *"showcasing"* a certain business for the month, so they hold the event at that person's place of business. This is perfect opportunity for exposing your business to the local community. I always enjoy seeing where and how a local business owner spends their day.

Some are scheduled at public venues, such as restaurants, taverns, country clubs, or hotel banquet facilities. In many cases these facilities can handle a larger number of participants. Holding events at some of the well-known and fashionable establishments draws a curious crowd as well.

Many of these gatherings in public or private locations are evening events, with most serving cocktails and food. A "No Host" bar is common.

The informal atmosphere tends to allow for a relaxing experience and encourage easy conversation. It is, what you make it. And some events might be held as morning mixers, or a midday lunch meeting. The basics are similar.

I have made some unexpected, and fruitful contacts because of the relaxed dynamics of social networking.

Social Networking or Business mixers, tend to be a stand-up type of affair with limited seating and several High-Top tables to encourage conversation. It's hard to ease into a conversation with people you don't know if everyone is sitting down at a dining table in groups. I'll explain more about this later in our networking journey.

There may, or may not be a featured Speaker. In some, more formal events, there will be time set aside for networking in a business expo format, and a twenty minute plus presentation, not only to advertise a sponsor, but to add to the educational interests of the audience.

Social networking can have a monetary cost or be complimentary. I always believe an event you pay for, should and usually does hold more value.

I once chaired a charity event for the Leukemia Society on Lake Mead in Nevada. It was a Sailing event hosted by our yacht club. Each year they had a Spectator Boat on the race course, so you could watch the race from the water. A huge houseboat, complete with food, soft drinks and booze. All at no charge. Any minimal donation allowed entrance to the Spectator Boat. The first three years not more than 6 people each year were on that boat.
Why? Because there was No Perceived Value.

The year I chaired the event I set a minimum amount. Even if you donated $10,000 dollars, to be on that spectator boat, you had to pay $35.00. That year we had 28 people aboard. Why? Because there was a Perceived Value. When it was free, nobody came, when we charged for it, everyone thought, WOW, only $35 dollars and we get to watch the race from the water, that's well worth it. When deciding on social networking events, think about what you get for free.

Some social networking clubs have an annual membership, some have a, pay as you go requirement, and some are complimentary with the cost being absorbed by the sponsors that pay to have their name advertised.

At many informal events you are also able to display your marketing materials such as brochures, business cards, or "swag" (company branded merchandise).

I often attend late afternoon business networking mixers where people gather to network before they head home. They usually begin around 5:00 pm. That's when people get out of work and can swing by before calling it a day. It can be sort of a buffer for them as well. Little meet and greet, wind down with comfortable conversation or vent to someone about their job.

Some seize the opportunity to meet other like-minded professionals to do some serious networking. I've looked at some events as I would a "<u>Professional Credits</u>" course. Many professionals have credit requirements to keep their licenses current. This was a way of keeping up on my game. How serious you want to take this is up to you.

And some, believe it or not, think it's a good opportunity to find a date. I've seen many people meet their new love at networking events, and others finding their soulmate.

The late afternoon or early evening mixers can reap some valuable rewards in many aspects, both in business and personal engagement.

Let's recap our points of interest on Social Networking.

- Usually non-structured, but still have an element for a planned agenda.
- Informal agenda.
- May have an educational interest.
- No accountability to attend.
- Non-consistent attendees.
- May have a minimal cost if any, or annual membership.
- May or may not have a featured speaker.
- No commitment to use anyone for business.
- Like minded individuals.
- Morning, lunch, or evening events.
- Evening events usually serve alcohol and food.
- Usually a Stand- Up Affair.
- May provide for attendees to put out marketing material.
- May be too informal to provide quality business.
- Relaxing atmosphere to unwind.
- Can build relationships through consistency.

Strategic Networking

Strategic networking events usually involve attending meetings within a given industry or field. Professional organizations that cater to Financial Advisors, Life Insurance professionals, Attorneys, and General Contractors, etc.

These types of industry organizations provide not only a networking aspect but an educational aspect as well. Usually scheduling informative Speakers presenting on products and services that enhance the professional's toolbox helping to learn new techniques on marketing and sales.

Strategic networking for Attorneys such as the State Bar Association can help discover new avenues of education and contacts for them and their industry.

I have been a member of our local Chamber of Commerce for many years. Using the programs and business networking opportunities that they've offered. Although their events can fall under Social Networking at times, they also act as the strategic networking we're talking about here. Some events planned were targeted for business education in the Financial arena, Real Estate, Construction, and more.

As a longtime Mortgage loan professional, I often attended for the learning experience from other professionals introducing new loan programs and financial benefits to borrowers.

I attended to hear the speakers approach. I listened to how the speakers presented their products, listening carefully on how I could present similar information in front of my audience on the education of mortgage financing.

A colleague of mine once told me that the education he received by attending some chamber workshops helped him to become a better public speaker and be a better listener.
This is a strategic approach in networking, because networking is not just about talking to people and making contacts, but it's about learning.

Strategic networking can be _You,_ attending a Speakers Forum. A Speaker's Forum can help you learn new skills on public speaking? Maybe you're not the type to get out in front of a crowd of 20, 50 or 150 people yet...... but you never know. What you have to say is important, let others hear how you can help them.

Not only are you practicing your presentation skills, but you're meeting some new people to connect with. And practicing the fine age-old art of speaking.

There are organizations that come together, for passing professional exams. Exams such as, Series 6& 63, and Series 7 (licensing for financial professionals). A collection of Insurance agents that gather to practice on taking exams for their insurance licenses and certifications. Again, another opportunity to meet more people that have information to share.

Yet another club that began as a Social Get-together, that eventually became a strategic networking group masterminding on each other's business challenges.

I was a member of an upscale private social club in Las Vegas. There was a lot of networking going on, and for many people, new long-lasting relationships formed. At one point I initiated a monthly lunch for selected business owners to come together and brainstorm what was working or not working for them in their business, and how each of us could help share our ideas. There were only six invited each month, at each luncheon I chose one attendee to express one major challenge happening in their business. What was challenging to them and how we can help.

Each of us, one by one asked questions of the chosen candidate. After the questions were done, we went around the table offering an idea or an experience that could help solve their issue. We did this for a little over a year until it dissolved. Why would such a good thing dissolve? It first was conceived just to get together and socially brainstorm our businesses, but quickly led to a more purposeful meeting with a specific agenda in mind. We started out socially, went to strategic, it was extremely beneficial but maybe, we should have added more structure for the ongoing stability.

We can learn so much by attending events such as informational programs. It doesn't always have to be in our specific field of business. That's the strategic part of what, I'm talking about here.

You can attend these events to either meet people that fall into your target market, or to meet people who are connected to your target market, these are bridges of Influence.

You never know who might show up offering advice or insight within your industry.

I was surprised a while back after attending an Attorney State Bar mixer that only about two thirds of attendees were Attorneys. The rest, were people that wanted to know, and acquire business from attorneys.

I remember hearing how Life Insurance agents would make connections on writing life insurance policies referred by Family Law Attorneys. Why? Because the spouse's attorney wanted to make sure the alimony that should get paid was protected, just in case the payee passed on.

This could be a great avenue for business if you're a Life Insurance Agent.

I was there as well while in the mortgage business, looking to network with some quality Family Law Attorneys so I could receive referrals on clients. Where else to meet the masses than at their own gathering hole.

As a home mortgage professional, I found it important to build a source of referrals through Family Law Attorneys. I realized during my career that when a married couple who owned a home was going through a divorce, both parties still needed a roof over their head.

This was the perfect opportunity to qualify each of them for a mortgage. One spouse might choose to stay in the house which resulted in a refinance, and the other many times wanted to go out and purchase their own home, spouse free.

They each needed a roof over their head and I was there to provide the financing.

With Divorce Attorneys on my radar I could possibly end up financing both properties; the one they're leaving, and the one they're buying.

This is true with Realtors as well of course, and many more types of industries.

Take a moment and think, what organizations can be a path to referring you clients. Think outside the box.

There are lot of resources that can come from strategically organizing your network.

Be conscious about discovering those opportunities. What organizations can you think of right now to attend?
Before reading on, take a moment and reflect on that.

A Life insurance friend of mine was a member of a local branch of the American Marketing Association. He was President of the chapter at one time.

What did Life insurance have to do with the members that were there learning about how their marketing companies could prosper?

It did Plenty. He met members that worked with business owners. Business owners that needed Life Insurance coverage, Disability Income, Buy/Sell Agreements, and many other business insurance needs. It was a very valuable resource for him. He made contacts that lasted for years to come.

Just being involved with even one organization creates more exposure for you.

I still have friends and business associates that deal with me. That I met through him, that he met through that association.

Strategic networking could involve many types of local chambers. There might be an Asian Chamber of Commerce, Urban Chamber of Commerce., Latin Chamber of Commerce. I even attended a Health & Wellness Chamber of Commerce.

As a Certified Professional Coach, I use an approach called Energy Leadership.

Energy Leadership is a unique approach which helps people to discover the default tendencies, beliefs, and perceptions they have adopted over the years. This helps them become conscious of how these default tendencies have guided their decisions and actions that has driven their business success, or lack thereof.

So, what does that have to do with the Health & Wellness Chamber of Commerce?

Wellness can take many forms. Physical, emotional, mental, spiritual etc. Energy Leadership deals with wellness in all those areas to keep you successful, in whatever your success belief is. It's all health in one form or another.

Many chambers have programs for members on learning opportunities in various industries, with classes and workshops.

These may include leadership programs, ribbon cuttings, and volunteers for local events.

Review all the available Chambers of Commerce within your area to see what services they offer to the public.

Organizations like chambers of commerce, service clubs, and philanthropic groups strategically arrange fundraisers and community efforts to raise money for a cause.

Service clubs such as Rotary groups, Kiwanis chapters. Non-Profit organizations such as St. Jude's, Leukemia Lymphoma Society etc. Their main purpose may not be for networking, but you may uncover untapped resources of business, and you will also feel good helping the community.

Strategic networking involves a lot of aspects of all types of networking. The educational aspects, the connections you make, and possibly discovering new avenues to go down to help in your local community, as we just discovered.

Before we cover the more detailed and complex world of Structured Networking,

Let's recap what I have shared in Strategic Networking.

- Usually structured.
- Formal or Informal agenda.
- Educational agenda.
- May or may not have a Keynote Speaker.
- Consistent attendees.
- May have a one-time attendance fee or membership fee.
- No commitment to use anyone for business.
- Like minded individuals.
- Familiar topics.
- May be Private or Public venue.
- May be at someone's place of business.
- May or may not serve alcohol and food.
- Usually not a stand-up Affair.
- Can build relationships through consistency.
- Little or no accountability to attend.
- Informal networking.
- Financial commitment.
- May be morning, afternoon or early evening events.
- May or may not provide for attendees to put out marketing material.

Structured Networking

Now we venture on Structured Networking, a more committed and accountable environment.

Structured Networking is commonly hosted by an organization that exists for the primary purpose of helping people network in a specifically planned setting, existing of exclusive business professionals.

Two of the largest networking organizations such as LeTip International and BNI (Business Network International) hold fast to the true model of structured networking. Most common businesses associated with these types of organizations include but are not limited to, The Real Estate profession, Insurance industry, Financial specialists, banking institutions, CPAs and multiple types of Contractors, inclusive of start-ups as well.

These fore mentioned professions tend to rely on word of mouth referrals to increase their client base making a structured networking group more valuable.

Members agree to practice loyalty to each other in the form of referrals. Loyalty meaning that they will refer their fellow members over another business in that industry. This loyalty factor helps keep the members thinking about each other when they notice their clients have a need to fill.

They usually allow only one business to be represented in their meeting group (or so-called chapter), so they eliminate competition among members. The strict compliance of one business category per chapter helps to increase the loyalty factor we spoke of.

Sometimes prospects attending these groups are hesitant to join because they have built allegiances to others and wonder now, how they can practice that loyalty. But it can be very beneficial as time goes by to build new relationships through this portal of committed professionals.

Most structured networking groups meet on a weekly basis usually in a public venue such as a restaurant or country club setting that provides a private meeting room. The weekly meetings help to solidify the relationships by having consistency. After meeting, week after week, month after month, it's hard to forget about each other. The weekly process helps to keep each member on each other's minds. When a friend, a client, a family member, mentions a need, the member of that group can't help but think about someone that can help fill that requirement.

The public setting allows for additional marketing. When patrons walk in and see a meeting going on, they sometimes wonder what it's about. They may be inquisitive about joining in at the meeting themselves.
.

When you're in a structured networking group, you become the Go-to-Person for everyone that knows you. When you are part of a solid referral group, people know it. They depend on you as a resource to put them in touch with someone that can help them. In turn, this helps your clients, rely on you.
The more your client thinks about you, the more referral business you can get from them.

I was in a structured business group called LeTip for many years holding the Mortgage Loan category. I became the Go-to-Person for my family, clients, and friends.

I can remember many times, when a client would call me up and ask for a recommendation on an Attorney, CPA, Chiropractor, etc.

Here is how that scenario would play out.

"John I'm looking for a good Financial Advisor, can you recommend someone". "Of course, I can". Her name is Denise so and so. Let me give you her phone number and email. I'll also forward your information to her and make sure she calls you within the next 24 hours or sooner".

"Thanks John".

"Hey John, by the way now that I have you on the phone, I just thought of a friend of mine having trouble getting financed would you mind calling him to see how you can help him".

Imagine, my client calls me for a recommendation, thinks for a moment, and turns out giving me a referral. This happened to me dozens of times because I am in a structured referral networking group. I am the Go-to-Person, it feels good. I can help my client in so many ways.

A structured networking group has a formal agenda. The meeting is organized, there is a desired purpose and you basically know what to expect.

The meeting may start off with meet and greet session before the formal agenda starts. The formal agenda may start with introductions of members and guests, moving on to committee reports from the club officers. A treasury report and most of the expected formalities of board member reports

Knowing there is a formal agenda and not just an Off-the-Cuff meeting, displays a professional and productive environment.

There usually is a Speaker of the Day. A member, or non-member educating the audience on their product or service. This is the opportunity to speak and educate the members on what you do and how they can help you. The more we know about each other, the more we can help each other. And the more you give the more you'll get.

The purpose of being in a structured networking organization is to rely on each other for quality business and learn from each other on how to do this.

Some groups only allow members, to do a presentation. The purpose here is to learn as much as you can about the member, so you can refer them easily when you're out in the marketplace.

Structured networking groups usually have an attendance requirement encouraging the members to be at the meeting consistently.

This not only keeps everyone on each other's mind, but also keeps the meeting room looking full. Having full membership at each meeting keeps the energy up and has a lot to say about the members.

It usually says, the members want to be there, not just because it's required.

It's hard to get enthused walking into a networking meeting with 4 or 5 people. It's more fun in numbers. So inviting guests that are eligible to join the group is significant to the chapters success.

Structured networking groups have a committed Board of Directors. A list of Officers responsible for the ongoing health of the chapter. These are the leaders making sure the rules and protocol are being followed. The Board of Directors know, they must set the example for the others. Leading by example will inspire the members.

Many people ask me what makes one group better or different than another. For years I tried to figure this out. I first thought it's the leadership, then I thought, no it's the makeup of the members, no maybe the location. But over time, I'm totally convinced, it's the leadership. Yes, the leadership no matter how you look at it makes all the difference in the world.

The Board Members, the officers, managers of companies, truly are the ones responsible for its success.

I founded and managed my own office cleaning company for over 9 years. I used to clean offices, did it myself. Emptied trash, mopped floors, dusted furniture, everything it took to satisfy my customers. I became so busy after a while, I had to hire an employee, then another, then another. There came a time when I had enough employees that I didn't have to go out and do the cleaning myself. I had my techs doing it. I procured many more accounts over time and managed the business. I had a lead employee that would supervise the jobs. I would go out and check on the crew at the buildings two to three times per week. There was never a time where I walked through the building looking at what they did without picking up a mop, emptying a trash can or helping to clean the toilets. You see, there was nothing I would have them do, that I wouldn't do myself. I led by example.

Officers of structured networking groups lead by example if it's to be successful.

Most structured networking organizations allow only one business category to be represented in a group or chapter. For easy reference I'll refer to them as chapters. Having one business represented allows for exclusivity and prevents competition among members of that chapter. Although some businesses may overlap, such as in the financial field, law firms or banks, it allows for more members, and in turn more people that know more people.

For example, many Life Insurance agents do financial services, and many Financial Advisors are licensed in Life Insurance. The two go hand in hand, but having similar professionals, in a chapter allows for more referrals for both parties.

Picture this, a Banker in a chapter, that does Business Banking, Financial products, Insurance, Commercial loans, Credit Card services, Payroll. That's one person knowing maybe 200 people. Now picture a Banker, Financial Advisor, a Life Insurance Agent, a Credit Card Merchant service individual, a Payroll Service representative. That's five people that probably know 200 people each. That's one thousand possible referrals for the Banker, or the Financial Advisor, or Life Insurance Agent, etc. Get the picture? You can imagine how much business and contacts can be going around that room each week. There's strength in numbers not to mention the intelligence of all those quality professionals. Imagine what can be learned there.

Of course, as professionals we have built allegiances over time with people we depend on, and now we are expected to practice loyalty to our new-found referral sources. Sometimes this can be a challenge, but most groups like the big structured networking organizations have educational programs that coach on learning how to navigate through these ethical tasks.

These could be challenges, or they could be opportunities, depending on how we look at it.

Most structured networking organizations have multiple chapters or clubs throughout the city, country, or world for that matter. Having this influence and recognition is an advantage to all the groups, whether small or large in numbers. Members have the advantage of using each other when a business is not already represented in their own specific group. This also allows for a business owner to have their partners or associates represented in other chapters associated with the same organization.

When I first joined the LeTip leads group I was a Sales Manager for a large payroll service in Nevada. I had four salespeople working for me. We had five LeTip chapters located in the Las Vegas area, so I put a representative in each chapter, locking up any opportunity for the competition to join. This is a huge benefit in belonging to a major structured networking organization such as LeTip International, BNI or Team Referral Network.

Structured networking groups are either morning breakfast meetings, or lunch time meetings held in a public venue, such as country clubs or restaurants that provide a private room for their meeting space. It's mostly a seated event with a mix and mingle moment before the official program starts.

The public venue allows for a bit of extra marketing. Patrons that visit the venue often want to know what the group is about. When I walk into my meetings I have a name badge on that includes the name of my networking group as well.

Members are usually held to a commitment of giving business. It's more of a give and get model. Although the key reason for joining is to get business, it starts with giving. If you fail to give business or show up, you could be asked to leave the group. Some people don't like that accountability, but structured networking is about commitment and accountability.

Structured groups usually have a fee to join and more than likely a monthly or quarterly fee to cover costs. This varies greatly from one organization to another. Some people tend to look at it as a cost and not as an investment. Like any marketing tool, there is an investment to market your business.

I'm not buying leads, I'm leasing relationships.

Relationships may take time to build, but they can last forever depending on how you take care of them. There's cost and there's value. The group may set the cost, but you create the value.

I look at it this way, if you don't have enough confidence to invest in your business, how can the members feel confident referring you to their most valuable clients.

Networking with likeminded professionals has its responsibilities.

Let's recap our key points for Structured Networking.

- Formal & structured agenda.
- You become the Go to Person.
- Board or committee in place responsible for the welfare of the organization.
- Member to member loyalty.
- May include an educational agenda.
- Exclusivity, only one business category allowed.
- Featured Speaker at meetings.
- Members held accountable.
- Accountability to attend.
- Accountability to provide business.

- Multiple groups throughout the city, country or world.
- Meet weekly.
- Consistent attendees.
- Financial commitment.
- Usually a membership fee.
- Like minded individuals.
- Familiar topics.
- Usually a public venue.
- May be at someone's place of business or public venue.
- Seated format.
- Usually morning or lunchtime meetings.
- Usually food is served.
- Opportunity to display marketing materials.
- Formality provides for a quality source of business.
- You build relationships through consistency.
- May have periodic evening events with food and alcohol.

Where Do We Network

Everyone tells me I need to be networking, but I don't know where to network.

So, where do we Network?

We covered a lot of information on the, What, the Why, the Types. Now, where to Network?

We touched on a few ideas previously. How do we know which events, which meetings, which brainstorming sessions will be fruitful for our growth and knowledge? Well.........We don't.

You need to research and explore. Exploring can be enlightening, and fun. Where to network for business will depend on many factors. What do I want to accomplish? What am I looking for? What specific businesses do I want to target? Will I feel comfortable with the surroundings? Are people friendly, or cliquish?

Let's take each networking opportunity step by step.

Chamber of Commerce.
Just about every city, town, or county has a Chamber of Commerce. What each chamber offers will depend

on its membership, size of the community, and overall purpose.

When I moved to southern Nevada, I wasn't sure what I was going to do to earn an income. I made a hasty decision based on frustration of my current job in New York City and our family's situation.

I worked on Wall St. as an Operations Consultant, contracted by financial institutions to research and solve departmental problems and create new departments for management. So, when my wife and I decided to move out west, we made a leap of faith not knowing what was to come.

We moved into her parent's house until we found our way. So, once I arrive in the bustling town of Las Vegas, I thought, where do I go to discover what businesses there are here in town.

The Chamber of Commerce I'm sure can be a start. I drove up to their office, went inside, and was met by a friendly community advocate showing me brochures of various businesses in town that they support.

I took brochures, pamphlets and business cards out of the rack. I asked questions. I hate to admit it, but I didn't even know what a Chamber of Commerce was.

All I knew was there were a lot of business cards and brochures sitting around.

I was in the process of setting up a Janitorial Business, and had no clue how I was going to do it, I just knew that I could. It's great when you don't know too much. It eliminates that barrier, that only gets in the way if you know it's there.

I soon started the business and became a member of the chamber just to meet people.

Again, I had no idea what the mission of the chamber was, all I knew was, I'm new in town and wanted to make some contacts.

I started volunteering on different committees. Committees that had to do with small businesses. I became a volunteer Ambassador for the chamber.

As an Ambassador I attended networking events that the chamber organized to greet members and guests at the door or work the room for them introducing members and guests to each other. Practicing the art of networking.

I volunteered on their new member committee, then on their government affairs committee. Later after a few years of living and breathing Las Vegas, I helped on a committee that welcomed new teachers into town by taking them to lunch or meeting for dinner with the purpose of helping them acclimate to the community and referring them to services in the community if they needed. It was a public relations effort, make them feel good about their decision to make Las Vegas their home.

This put me out to the community. People knew my name, my business and my values that I live by. Anything to be involved in the community.
It wasn't who I knew, but who knew me.

People remembered me and respected the fact that I volunteered. It kept me busy....... Busy meeting people and solidifying contacts. I had no idea for the next 24 years I would still be networking through the chamber. The chamber was one of the major relationship building opportunities I used at first.

Chambers of Commerce usually work on a thin budget, so they welcome and encourage volunteers.
There are departments for community service, such as, Ribbon Cuttings, Business Affairs, Leadership Education, monthly networking breakfasts, power lunches, New member breakfast or lunches, monthly luncheons with keynote speakers.

One thing you can be sure of, everyone is there for the same reason, to meet, greet and be involved with like-minded individuals.

You'll hear me say this time and time again,

It Is, What You Make It.

Look in to your local chamber. It's not too pricey, and it can make a world of difference if you work it right.

So where do we go next on a networking journey?

Service Organizations

How about Service Organizations, like Kiwanis, Rotary chapters, ethnic groups.

Ethnic groups.

What do you think about that? They are not specific leads groups, but they can be very valuable in meeting others that have grown up with the same culture and similar experiences.

Another organization I gravitated to as soon as I arrived in Las Vegas, was the **Italian American Club**. It was a natural for me since I was a second-generation Italian-American, and from a city environment.

I wanted to be close to people that had the same mind set as me, the same way of speaking. Although we all spoke English, some a little broken English, we had language accents associated with the neighborhoods we grew up in.

I joined the Italian American Club cause I wanted to be with people that understood where I came from, what kind of food I ate, and where I ate it.

I found out later what a great networking opportunity it was as well. Certain ethnic groups like to do business with their own kind. They feel a close connection. This has nothing to do with any prejudice, it has to do with familiarity, a language of understanding. We know it well being part of a country of immigrants in America.

Right away I was accepted and given a chance. One of our members always practiced using a member for any services they needed. He felt that just being part of our club you deserved the opportunity to be given first choice. If you did the job right, you earned a new friend and a client for life. If you didn't, you were still a friend just not a client.

Think about where you fit in?

Other service organizations are Kiwanis and Rotary clubs.

These clubs have a mission to help in community efforts. The **Kiwanis club** empowers communities to improve the world by making lasting differences in the lives of children. Further mission statement is to be a positive influence in communities worldwide – so that one day, all children will wake up in communities that believe in them, nurture them and provide the support they need to thrive. In the United States around the 4th of July Holiday, the Kiwanis organization sets up temporary stands to sell fireworks to raise funds for community efforts.

The **Rotary club** is a similar organization that usually provides money and fundraisers to donate in needy cases. The mission of Rotary International is to provide service to others, promote integrity, and advance world understanding, goodwill, and peace through its fellowship of business, professional, and community leaders.

This is a powerful mission statement holding its members accountable. You would think their integrity holds true to their business and reference to each other, and it does just that. It's influential networking.

In my experience with Rotary and Kiwanis chapters, I always found the members to have a high regard for each other. They commit to a strict code of ethics that binds them together.

I recall one small city I visited where I attempted to open a business leads group only to find, just about every business person was a member of the local Rotary. More than a good old boy network, the whole town was in their membership. I wanted to move there just to be in their group.

Again, they're not formed for business leads, but they are formed to network and support.

Let's visit a few more areas of where to network.

Recreational Clubs.

What I mean by recreational clubs are the clubs and sports you enjoy outside of your job. Your, out of career activities.

What sports do you enjoy? Tennis, Volley ball, Fishing, Hiking, Sailing, motorcycling, long walks on the beach.

There's activities for everyone, and we can utilize them to network for our business subliminally.

If you enjoy the sport of Tennis, don't just go to play, be involved with the tennis community.

I enjoy sailing, so I join a sailing club. I get so much out of the club, emotionally, spiritually, physically and financially. In the Mortgage business we used to choose our Home Appraisers. I had an appraiser I used for quite some time., and while, one day sitting around with a sailing acquaintance at the lake, I happened to ask him what business he was in.

Turned out he was a Home Property Appraiser. Just the guy I could do business with. I used him on many occasions when I was in the middle of a loan transaction. In turn, I received some well, deserved business referrals from him as well. My sailing club for fun, turned into financial satisfaction as well.

A situation happened to me years back when I first learned to sail.

As many of you may know, when you look at a sailboat, there is a long pole sticking up from the middle, there are many wires that hold up that pole. Well if one or more of those wires break then the pole finds it hard to stay upright,

One bright breezy afternoon while out sailing, one of the main stays that helped hold up my mast broke, damaging the deck of the boat and the mast practically falling into the water. A scary situation in the least.

I managed to get the boat back into the slip wondering what the heck I was going to do with a broken boat.

Well, since I was a member of this great recreational club, The Nevada Yacht Club, I had a lot of resources to rely on. To make a long story short. Sailor after sailor offered suggestions on repairs, and I was able to get my boat back on the water sailing after only a couple of months. Without the ability to network within the club I may not have had the expertise of many others to offer help. This is still networking whether you think you are doing it or not.

Not just in business, but in what we do day after day.

Building relationships is networking even outside of work. And you still never know what business comes from it. Where we network, has to do with many activities we do day in and day out. It's not always business to business, but the information we exchange, makes us smarter, more compassionate, and connects us socially as well.

How about Golf? Where else do we hold each other hostage for four to five hours. What a great networking opportunity. They're stuck with you.

How much information can be shared spending time on the green with one to three other people.

They say more business gets consummated on the golf course than any other type of activity. Very true.

When you finish my book, take up golf if you haven't already.

Let me ask you, what opportunities do you see in the recreational activities that you do? Who do you rely on within the clubs you're attached to both financially and personally?

How about your child's sports activities? Soccer, baseball, basketball, high school sports. These are networking opportunities too. Who did you stand next to? What else do you have in common? Do you ever get together with the other parents after the game?

Both my son and daughter played sports. We've spent many evenings and weekends watching games, conversing with the other parents, and many times breaking bread with them at a restaurant after the game. That's another way to casually network.

I've formed many friendships connecting with my children's friend's parents. Again, networking is building relationships.

Many of you parents out there can attest to the fact that a lot of your friends today actually came about from your children.

Other Places to Network

How about Church? Do we network on a Sunday morning, sure we do, Go ahead, admit it?

Big one......... Charity Events, Fundraisers. Who goes to fundraisers? Usually successful people. People with financial means. People that want to give back to the community.

Start with the Why. Why am I really, here? It must be authentic. Business will end up happening eventually. Get involved with a charity you feel passionate about.

We network everywhere. I travel often. So, when I go out for dinner by myself, where do you think I sit? At the Bar section of the restaurant. I feel uncomfortable sitting alone at a dining table in a restaurant. If I sit at the Bar I get to talk to people. Yes, they're strangers, but they're usually alone too, maybe on business as well. They may want some friendly conversation, they may want to educate me on their product or service too.

My wife and I go out alone for dinner quite often. Unless we're feeling for a romantic candlelight supper, we sit at the Bar or in the Bar area at a High-Top table. That's where we meet people and generate interesting conversation with other couples.

We like learning about others and exploring what others think and feel. Meeting new people is networking, not for business, just for socializing.

Sometimes it turns into new friendships, sometimes it turns into new business. You can network anywhere.

Recreational clubs, service organizations, religious services, evening networking events, whether social, strategic or structured.

High school activities, public venues for dinner, golf, chambers of commerce, our children's sports, fundraising events.

Where do we network? **In our frame of mind.**

Social on-line Networking

Other Networking opportunities include the *social online networking* activities. At the writing of this book, our current online resources: Google, Meetup, LinkedIn, Yelp & Facebook. This is by no means a complete list, but just about now the most popular.

Online social media changes constantly. Let's first look at **Google**.

When you *Google search something* like "business networking locally", You'll find a vast array of networking opportunities suggesting social events, networking groups, exclusive and non-exclusive networking opportunities. Events happening in the morning, in the evening, luncheons and Happy Hour get togethers.

You'll find structured and unstructured organizations. Check out their websites. Not all the groups you review will fit your needs. Research the people involved. Who are they, and what business are they in. Don't believe everything you read. Go by your instincts, they're usually right.

You'll find **Meetups**, where networkers get together for specific challenges happening in their lives. Many networking groups advertise their own meetings on Facebook. At the time of this writing, the **Meetup** website is extremely popular. This site is just as it sounds, Lets M*eet- up*. The site offers every type of interest from Hiking groups to emotional support.

If there is a special interest you are passionate about, inquire within and see what it has to offer you, both in business and personal gratification. You can find just about everything you're looking for there.

LinkedIn is another site, specializing in more "business" than "non-business" networking. Online networking promotes you and your business, however we may or may not recognize people on there. It's a good platform for getting exposure and keeping your name out in the marketplace.

It also offers a network into, Job offers and notifications when people want to connect with you.

You may or may not get substantial closed business. There is an element of education and information offered by the members that can be useful. It's still a worthwhile site to have a presence.

Yelp is another useful site for testimonials. Members sign on and recommend people they know. This can be used as an opportunity to review how many accolades someone gets and in turn be someone you may want to network with. It's a head start on getting to know someone.

Let's say you want to network with a good Commercial Realtor to recommend to your clients or form a reliable business relationship, it may be worth the effort to set up a time to meet in person and learn how the two of you can share information with each other.

Yelp can provide you with a large list of professionals you may want to build a power team with. You can start your own dynamic networking group relying on each other for business leads and begin building longstanding relationships from there.

Try pulling together the businesses that you are most likely to give business to and get business from.

As far as the recommendations on quality, that you will have to assess yourself.

Facebook is another on-line network. It's amazing how many people you get to see and hear about. Friends, family, business associates and many more. This is another place to market yourself in several ways. It's a virtual billboard on a major freeway, and there's loads of traffic.

To find referral sources you can simply announce what you're looking for. Your message goes out to thousands. Try asking for a good referral source to introduce to your clients and associates. Whatever business you're in, announce that you would like to meet up with a referral source close to your community. Of course, these are already friends or acquaintances and should be a safe environment, but always be cautious of who you meet on line. Meet in a public place, or better yet, decide on a local business mixer to meet at.

Meeting at a business mixer gives you both the opportunity to be in a place with many other business associated individuals and have the prospect of opening up more contacts.

Facebook can also be used to include video clips and pictures emphasizing your business's features and benefits.

It's so easy to capture our moments these days with cameras and video on our smartphones. Anytime you're giving a presentation, or making a short speech have someone video or snap some photos of you.

This is another opportunity to add or post to your social media. How many times have you seen this done with others, and you probably keep saying I should do that. If you're not doing it now, start.
Its free advertising and keeps you in the minds of whoever is visiting the same websites you are.

Social media is nice source, and everything has a place for how we want to advertise and connect with others.

Make your own list of what on-line sites you can get noticed and connect with other like-minded professionals.

There are many sites offering members a list of qualified professionals that have been recommended.

I was never sure if these testimonials were factual. I have seen people go online and write a review for a business just to win a prize or receive a coupon offer. At times its people wanting others to recommend them. I have found the traditional "face to face" networking more effective in turning into closed business.
Now of course this will depend on the type of business you're in.

A florist for instance will do very well on an informational site such as this, however, a Financial Advisor responsible for someone's financial future may get genuine qualified referrals from someone personally recommending them. To me the real referral is someone verbally recommending me and telling a prospect how I have personally helped them. Sounds a little old fashion in this era of technology, but I feel, as long as if we are human, we will be using our minds to think, our mouths to speak, and our ears to listen.

Preparing to Network

Now that we have discovered several areas of where to network, how do we prepare?

Here we will focus on networking face to face.

So, you're attending a business networking event, let's discuss preparing.

What type of event is it? We discussed the typical business networking mixer, so we'll go with that scenario.

How about timing? At times, we are heading to a networking mixer from our place of business. Consider the travel time, how long will it take to get there. What time does it start?

Some people feel more comfortable when there is already a crowd.?

If that's you, get over it.

Start making the events as if it's, your event. If you're one of only a few people already there, stand at the entrance and say hello. This can help you feel more comfortable rather than standing alone inside a room where you don't know anyone, or don't know what to say to break the ice to the few that are there.

It's an easier ice breaker standing at the entrance just to say hello to anyone that walks in. Even a nod of the head or a smile can get their attention.

You might even ask at the registration table if they would like help greeting the everyone. What a wonderful way to be able to introduce yourself to everyone that walks in.

If you attend many of the same sponsored events you may notice the same people are always there early. What this tells me is they are enthused about being there and serious about meeting everyone.

Preparing to network could involve reviewing a list of the attendees.

Who is involved with the event, are they members of the organization. Depending on type of business mixer, you may have access to the attendee list. If there is an organized membership, who are the members? What type of businesses are they in? Who would fall into your target market? You may find you already are familiar with some of people attending.

Knowing a little bit about the organization that hosts the event, can offer you some insight on the type of businesses attending as well. After showing up at some of the same mixer events, you'll have an idea of which business professionals attend steadily.

It's a good habit to get into checking some info on the internet of the kinds of businesses that attend which kinds of mixers.

Some may have a good amount of sales people, such as Life Insurance, Realtors etc. some may have a large following of Multi-Level Marketing (MLM) businesses.

At times I'll search the internet to see what the organization has done in the past. I like to look at pictures of their past events to get an idea of who shows up. Knowing who has shown up before gives me an idea if I want to attend at all.

If it is a Fundraiser event, be prepared with a credit card or check book. Many of these events will have a silent auction, and other ideas on how to have the attendees reach into their pocket to fund their cause. There's no obligation to donate, and they may not notice you *not donating*, but they will more than likely notice you, when you are a donor. Consider the effect when you are noticed.

No matter which event you chose to network at, consider your purpose for being there, Is it constructive.

Don't spend too much time speaking with one interesting person. You have more of you that can be beneficial to others as well. Try not to let one person take up all your time.

Clothing.
What to wear? What's appropriate for the occasion?

Where is the event. A Country Club, Restaurant, business office. As I mentioned previously, reviewing past photos can be very helpful. Previous events can help you decide on what the proper attire might be.

You want to fit into the crowd.

While attending business networking events you'll notice some people in Suit and Tie, some in sport jackets with an open color shirt or the old Miami Vice looks, if you know what I mean – Jacket, slacks and tee shirt. Some more casual in their logo golf shirts and kaki's, and others in stylish, or not so stylish jeans.

Just be comfortable in what you wear.

When the crowd is dressed down, let's say in less than business casual, if you're wearing a nice suit and tie, you will get noticed.

I had an invitation to a business networking event a while back at a Las Vegas Hotel. Poolside.... Poolside, what does that mean?

It was summertime, hotel pool, but a business networking event. Sure, the invite read, comfortable poolside attire, but what does that mean. Shorts, cabana shirt, were some guys coming in sandals? This was probably the one-time women did not have to worry about what to wear. They could be comfortable in a sundress and sandals or light slacks I imagine.

Now I'm used to dressing for business, somewhat formal. I usually wear a suit, many times a tie. But most of the time a suit and a crisp open collar shirt. I usually feel underdressed without a sport jacket or suit jacket during business hours. So, you'll usually see me in one or the other.

I contemplated for a bit. Shorts? nice shorts? Man, what if no one has shorts on but me. I knew a jacket and tie was overkill. But jacket or no jacket?

I took a chance way against my grain, I wore nice casual light slacks, beige, a light matching shirt worn outside the pants, or as we say Untucked. And then, totally not me, attending a business networking event, a nice pair of dark brown sandals. For those that know me in business, seeing me in jeans while doing business is a bit out of character for me. So, the sandals thing was a real stretch. But then I thought, I look cool, don't many movie celebrities dress like this, sure they do.

Again, it was spring in the Mojave Desert just prior to the Summer season. Hottest part of the day, 5:00pm. Temperature about 85-90 degrees. When I arrived, I said hello to a couple of business people I know, of which one of them was wearing a nice pair of shorts with fashionable sandals, seemed okay to me.

Another couple of guys wearing shirts and no jackets. After meeting a greeting for a while, I observed some dudes in business suits and thought, I'm glad I thought about my clothing choice. You see I was comfortable in what I was wearing. Not overdressed or underdressed, and therefore, I felt more confident. When I was more confident, I seemed to project better, and whether others were receiving me well or not, it didn't matter because I was comfortable, and I was confident.

Now some guys may not be as particular as I am about their clothing, but it's just me. To me it made a difference.

Proper dress is important in business. Whether it's because others expect business attire, or whether it's just dressing down to meet your audience.

These days, males can usually be comfortable in a suit or sport coat and open collar shirt. Females can get away with a lot more, whether it's a pant suit, dress or casual skirt, they can usually hit the mark.

I recall facilitating one specific business leads group that was meeting in the morning each week for breakfast. The members were business professionals, Attorneys to Auto Mechanics and many businesses in between. I remember the challenge I had when I approached the person that was leading the meetings. He was a good speaker, passionate about getting the group off to a good start. He was rather large, roundish gent, only about 5' 7" in height, but well over two hundred pounds.

He usually wore a golf shirt and kakis with sneakers. Unfortunately, his appearance made a negative impression on some of the members.

They felt if he was to stand at the head table running the meetings, he should be a little more professional in his dress. I agreed. Now it wasn't the fact of the golf shirt and kaki's, many people look just fine in that attire, but again, he was about 5'7' a good 200 plus pounds with a big round gut. The casual appearance didn't work well for the members. A nice professional suit could have made all the difference in the world where he could have commanded the room in a professional manner.

What I'm explaining here is that some people look great in a tee shirt and skinny jeans, and some just don't. Think about your dress when addressing an audience. What impression are you looking to make? What's the vision you want them to remember later in the day. Be appropriate for the environment you're networking in.

Now take the pool scenario. Females should understand, what is appropriate for business and what is appropriate for gaining productive attention. Being too exposed is great for getting people to notice you, but what are they noticing.

So, for females the proper dress goes a little bit further. Always consider what you want people noticing. Usually you want them concentrating on your eyes, because they're closer to your brain.

Business Cards.

How many business cards do you have? Did you replenish your supply? Are they easy for everyone to read?

I have been given some business cards where I have trouble reading the print such as the email, phone number or even their name. You may be at a Young Professionals network event, but some older attendees may have a little trouble with fancy hard to decipher print.

Now this could be looked at either way. Hard to read, maybe they're spending more time looking at your card, or don't even bother because it's too hard to read.

Observe as many business cards as you can while out networking. Think about the colors and the print. The boxing, the weight of the paper, the cut of the corners. What you like about other people's cards is what others may like about yours. Have a professional design the image you want to portray.

Consider having two forms of business cards. Fancy, expensive ones, and everyday use. If you're in a networking group that meets weekly, you probably go through hundreds of cards in just a couple of months. You may want to have the fancy ones for those special occasions. Just like your mother putting out the good dishes for the holidays.

Many times, I'll see friends and associates I know over time redo their business cards. But only a handful that I observe keeping both styles on hand ready to give out. Depending on who they meet and what the situation is, will determine which business card they present.

Some people may combine many facets of their business on one card, and they may keep a more specific card with one field of expertise for handing out at other times.

People notice business cards. And they notice them more, when they are cheaply produced. You're not saving money by using cheap inexpensive business cards. Spend the money on yourself. Your business card is your calling card, it's your image.

What do you want it to say about you?

I have collected some pretty, awesome business cards. You can tell, time, effort, and expense went into them. By the way, those are the ones I keep. They hang around my desk and office because they deserve the time to be there. They also remind me of the person that gave it to me.

Think about the business cards you have collected over time. What do you remember about them? Was it the graphics, the color? Was there a self-portrait, a picture, some emotional invoking scene that struck you?

I use two different, style cards. I keep one style in my left pocket of my jacket, and the other card in the opposite pocket. I keep the cards I collect in yet another pocket. This helps streamline my conversation with someone when I don't have to fidget around juggling my business cards or someone else's.

Some people keep some note taking materials with them. A small spiral flip over the top note pad is helpful when you hear something that's important to you. We always thing we'll remember it, and, later well, you know..........

Prepare your questions.

For some people opening, or keeping a business conversation is challenging. For others it comes naturally, but like most things, we can learn by practicing.

I am not one of those guys that can keep talking and talking without a que. What I mean by that is some people just keep going on, non-stop. For someone like me, I need a starting point. You may be the same way. So, I work on asking questions to keep a conversation going.

I ask questions like What target market are you shooting for? Who in your business is your top competitor? Where do you network now for business? How do you stack up, and what makes you different?

Authentic complementing is a good start as well. "I like that suit". "Nice Tie". "Who does your hair"? What a nice color. You get the picture.

Don't let the fear of draining yourself to be there, hinder you from attending and being successful at networking events.

At business mixers it's very natural to just walk up to someone, ask their name, and introduce yourself. That's why they're there, it's expected.

Seriously think about what questions you might ask individuals in certain industries. Remember it's not about you at this point, it's about them. Asking lots of questions gives you knowledge, and makes them feel important.

You can also ask what brought them into their chosen career. What do they best about what they do? There's a story there, and they may want to tell it.

If someone is in the Insurance field, you can come up with something that pertains to your experience. Think about maybe a loss that happened. When you're familiar with a loss, you may have some questions that a professional can answer for you.

The more questions you ask, the more knowledgeable you become.

Elevator Speech
How's your **elevator speech**? Tell me in 30 seconds what you're about?

What is an elevator speech?

An **elevator speech** is a clear, brief message or "commercial" about you. It communicates who you are, what you're looking for and how you can benefit a company or person.
It's typically about 30 seconds, enough time to get someone interested, but not too much to turn them off.

The **purpose of an elevator pitch** is to interest the audience in continuing to talk. Gain interest in you, and ask questions.

If you're part of a structured business networking group, you probably practice your elevator speech every time your group gets together for a meeting.

It's a way to practice, time and time again how to present to others. But you're not just training yourself how to get better at delivering your elevator speech, you're also educating others on how to deliver it for you.

Consider having more than one quick elevator speech in your toolbox. Depending on the person you're talking to, you may want something that targets their industry. Or you may feel their natural energy and want to tap into that. Your instincts will help you there. Go by your gut.

If you're not sure if a certain approach will be received well, you're probably right, be prepared to change it up.

Your elevator speech is like your business card. It's your first impression. What does it say about you? First, keep industry jargon out of your introduction. Business professionals may be great at what they do, but if you are talking in your own language, make sure they speak it as well.

I hear many Realtors mention REO's. I happen to know what an REO is because I was in the Real Estate industry, but many intelligent business owners may not know that language. An REO is "Real Estate Owned" property, or bank owned, usually a property that has been foreclosed on. As a Realtor, you may know this, but others may not. And if they don't ask you to clarify by what you mean, then you've lost that audience.

Always clarify what you do. Be specific especially if you're not in a popular business. Obviously, a Realtor, an Insurance agent or Carpet Cleaner may be self-explanatory, but you can still WOW them.

Many people start with their great customer service, or their competitive pricing as well as how long they have been in business. Try sharing your experience as to why you chose the field you're in. Let them know your story. Think about why you're in your business. How did you get there? What events in your past affected you, that brought you to where you are right now? Sharing your story may be more memorable.

For example: If you're a Realtor: Did you know a very successful Realtor when you were younger and wanted to be like him or her, helping people find the home of their dreams? Is that why you chose that profession. Your story may be more interesting than why you're the best in the business.

I had a disappointing experience years ago when my wife and I were applying for our first home mortgage.

The loan officer kept hounding us for paperwork we either gave him already, or giving us a new list of things we needed. He changed our loan program midway into the deal causing us to come up with more money out of pocket than we originally expected. I thought to myself, how could this guy be making a living doing loans. How can he be putting people through this aggravation and heartache? It wasn't fair to do business the way he was doing it, so I chose to go into the mortgage loan business, so others don't have to be subject to such unprofessionalism like this guy I'm speaking of.

That's my Why,

Get Comfortable Networking

You don't have to go it alone. Invite a friend. When you schedule to attend a business mixer, think about who can come along with you. One good reason is accountability. Now someone is expecting you to be there with them as well. If you're feeling a little apprehensive about going, knowing someone may be waiting, will encourage you to attend.

Having a networking partner with you can help build your confidence in preparing to talk to strangers.

If you're a little intimidated on what to say, who to talk to, your networking buddy can help you warm up. Now you have someone you feel comfortable speaking with. You can start building on a conversation. This can be your shill, showing others there is some action going on with you. You're not alone. Someone may want to get into your conversation and introduce themselves,
now they make the first move.

You and your partner may strategize on who to talk to. What business professionals look interesting? You may see people you know, or people your partner knows.

Survey the room. Where's the crowd? Where's the Bar. Maybe that's where the crowd is. At the start of some networking events, the Bar is usually the first place, people gravitate to. A nice cocktail to take the edge off and start conversation.

Where's the appetizers? What type of people are hovering around the food? Either way, you'll notice conversation abundant in both these locations.

High Top tables make for the best networking opportunities. You can stand across from each other and still have a buffer in between for comfort such as laying down your drink, or food plate. You can politely intrude into a conversation when standing at a High-Top table. It's easy to say Hi.

Picture two or three people standing around a High-Top table. Simply walk over. You can respectively ask a question to the effect of, "may I" "Do you mind", as in asking may I stand here, or, do you mind if I rest my drink on this High-Top table so I can take part in you conversation.

When you look around the room, notice which table you want to intrude on. Again, that's why they're there, to engage.

This may be a little insensitive, but I always observe the Exits in case of an emergency. Can't hurt to be prepared when in a public venue with lots of people and something dramatic occurs.

Now that you and you buddy are comfortable, split up. Remember you're there to network and build new relationships, so don't take up too much of each other's time. Make the break and meet new people.

What may happen from attending the same type of networking group over and over is that you and your buddy may end up with circle of familiar friends at these events each time. Now, new relationships form. But don't get too comfortable with the same people, always meet and greet new potential referral sources. That is why you started to attend in the first place.

Food and Drink
Food or no food?

Many evening mixers supply appetizers.

So, do you feel comfortable eating? Personally, I don't care for eating at business mixers that offer spicy little meatballs or messy appetizers.

The foods put out can sometimes be....., well....., smelly, or play havoc with your breath. If I have bad breath at a business mixer, I probably don't know it. I may have some idea if nobody wants to speak to me, but I don't like to bet on this.

I keep away from many foods at networking events. However, to play it safe I'll indulge in crunchy veggies or fruits that can satisfy my hunger and keep a healthy mouth, such as apples, carrots, and celery.

You may be thinking, this is little over the top, but really think about it next time you're at mixer. Who were the ones you didn't enjoy speaking with?

If you're very hungry and choose to eat, arrive early enough to indulge before most people get there, so you can satisfy your hunger and still enjoy mixing and mingling without continually wiping the food from your mouth.

What about just shaking hands? You want to shake hands with the person you just met, be aware of the foods you are handling so you can meet and greet with a full outstretched hand. It's hard to say hello when you have a plate, and utensils in your hands. Yes, we sometimes do the Elbow Shake when necessary.

Having food at a networking event works in your favor when you have finished a conversation and want an excuse to move away. It's an easy out. "Nice meeting you, I'm going to grab a little more to eat, or drink, see you later".

Now this sounds a little gross but, did you ever have someone accidentally spit food in your drink while you're talking to them. Yes, it's a big turn off for me and may be for others. I'm not saying don't eat, but be conscious of how you are being received. I don't mean to scare you off, just be aware.

I might mention also, if you're hosting your own event at your office, or another type of venue, pay attention to the food plan. Having easy and clean items on the menu can have a positive remembrance to the affair.

Getting back to the Bar. Check before you go, is it a No Host Bar, which means you pay for the alcohol, or are drinks included. It may be Beer and Wine, or a Full Bar which may or may not have the Top Shelf stuff.

If it's a No Host bar, do they accept Credit Cards, or should I bring cash? If you intend to buy a round for some new-found friends, you'll want to be prepared.

Nothing worse than offering and not having the means.

Marketing Materials, Swag

Some business mixers allow you to lay out marketing materials. Make sure before you attend an event you inquire what is acceptable.

In many cases, networking events may be sponsored.

To offset the cost of the function, the hosting party may look to businesses for sponsorship.

Usually those sponsors will have the biggest displays or the only displays.

There may be one major sponsor, or several.

These are the ones that get to lay out marketing materials, such as brochures, promotional items.
They may also have air time, meaning they get to speak at the event or at least some time slot to promote themselves verbally.

In most cases if you're not a sponsor, you probably won't have the chance to hand out your own brochures. However, paid membership organizations may give their members the opportunity to lay out advertising pieces.

If you do have the opportunity, bring items people can use. Check with your advertising specialist on the hottest swag gifts.

Consider sponsoring business mixers yourself. This is an awesome opportunity to bring attention to yourself, and let the public know you're involved with the event. You're someone to be recognized and spoken to. Take notice every time you're at a business mixer as to what is happening so you can plan your own.

When at a mixer, don't forget a reliable pen so you can take notes. You may want to remember certain details about someone you have spoken to, or take a note on how interested they were in your product or service. They may give you some detailed information on something you want to write down, so it is also good to have a small spiral notebook available.

In some cultures, like the Asian culture, it is rude to write on someone's business card, so be aware when accepting a business card and the care they have taken in presenting it to you.

Show the same respect when handing them yours.

If I am going to write on someone's business card in front of them, I always ask first if they mind that I make a note on their card. It's a courtesy I like to show.

Now, that I have said that, here is when I will write something on their business card and usually when they not around.

When I am at a business mixer, I like to rank the person I have spoken to on how interested they are in my service.

When someone shows an interest in attending my workshops or networking chapters, or any other part of my business offered, I want to remember how interested they were, so I use a numbering system of 1 thru 5. If they are extremely interested and want more information, I write a number 5 on their card. Somewhat interested, I may write a 2 or 3. I want to remember a little about them, so I want to keep a note of where I met them, or maybe who we both know. We think we'll always remember, and the time comes where we say, I should have wrote it down.

Engaging in conversation as we briefly discussed earlier can be work. So, there is work in networking. Like a journalist, we're always on during an interview. Sometimes, working a business mixer can be like that. Be truly interested in what the person is telling you. If you have trouble staying interested, find one thing, and try hard to find that one thing that can keep you engaged in the conversation until you are ready to excuse yourself.

Identify

Remember who you spoke to. As we mentioned before, use a note taking system.

What's memorable about them?

Think about someone you work with, an associate, a client. Clearly see them in your mind. What's memorable about them? What color is their hair? What do they wear? Are they animated when they speak, or dry? Excitable or calm? How's their laugh? Maybe certain shoes, laces or loafers, high heal shoes or flats. When your speaking with someone at a networking event, it's nice to remember them when you see them next time. They are always impressed when you remember them, even more so when you remember their name. When you can do this, you make them feel special, and they will also remember you.

Now let's Identify the opportunity of working with them. Have we identified their resources? Who do they know? Who do they use within their own networking circles? How do they get their business?

We may have mentioned this before, but knowing how someone gets their business, can be a powerful conversation piece. When we know their allies, we can strategize a game plan for building a net, of mutual referrals sources.

Discover where they hang out. The people you're talking to at mixers have other interests. Identify what these interests are. What are their hobbies and recreational activities. What charity groups are they passionate about. Maybe you have the same interest. Find out how you can participate in theirs. Networking is building relationships through trust and nurturing.

Be Valuable

You just made a friend. What do you know about him or her. Don't feel embarrassed to ask questions about them or their business. Be inquisitive. Truly be interested in who they are, what they do. What excites them, and where is their passion.

We talk about giving. The more you give, the more you shall receive. Nothing has ever been truer than that phrase. Being valuable can be as simple as listening to what their business is about. Concern for their challenges.

Maybe someone is standing alone not sure how to break the ice with others. How valuable can you be to that person at that given moment. It's not like you're asking them to dance. No shame in going over and saying hello. Imagine that person is your next biggest client. Identify people that you can relate to.

I mentioned having a friend to accompany you at a business mixer. This could be a convenient time to introduce that person around. Maybe you're talking to someone and an acquaintance walks over. You introduce each other, and another potential friendship is initiated.

Many a time when I have been talking with people and someone walks over to say hi. Right away I'm quick to introduce each other and mention their business. Maybe in conversation something came out that gave me the opportunity to connect one with the other on some prospective business.

I like to let others know that I have used someone before, and they as well might be able to retain their services.

Hype up anyone you know that may be able to service their needs. If you trust the person you are referring, others will trust you. It doesn't always work out, but nothing is guaranteed.

Follow Up

Follow up is key to building that relationship. How many people do you meet that say, I'll call you. We'll get together, and you never hear from them. You've forgotten about them, and they have forgotten about you. At least till you see them at another networking event.

It takes discipline to follow up, but you need to do it.

What do you do after you leave that business mixer?

Now you have a couple dozen business cards. You may have notes written on a few. Make use of it, no matter how busy you get. First chance you get in front of your computer, log in their info. Send a note.

There are many CRM (Customer Relationship Management) programs that can help with this. Some are very specific, complex and costly, but even purchasing a small business card reader can get you started. Inquire within your local office supply outlet on what inexpensive but valuable software products are available.

How about the many business professionals you are already meeting while you're networking?

A helpful conversation starter for any salesperson might be, "how do you track your prospects and clients"? An approach like this can turn into a treasured lesson for you. Not only that, but the person you ask that happens to use those resources, feels empowered by educating you. What a way to make someone feel special.

If you tell someone you will send them something, or contact them....... do it.

Following up can be as simple as a short email letting them know it was nice speaking with them. It doesn't have to be long, just enough so they remember you exist.

If you're going to set a time to meet for lunch, coffee, whatever, have your dates available and propose, two or three timeslots, that you can commit to.

I have heard, and said so many times in the past, "let's get together", and it never happens. Even though we have said it over, and over again to the same person, seeing them at the same event, it goes by the wayside. This happens a lot, and that's like making a sales call and not asking for the business.

Think of it this way. If that person said let's get together, I want to give you a $100,000 deal, packaged and ready to go, you would undoubtedly arrange it immediately.

It's a mindset. It's discipline, and that means it needs to be a practiced. Make it a habit to follow up.

I'm more surprised when I meet someone at a networking event and the next day, or even that very evening I receive a <u>"Nice to meet you"</u> email. I think that's great. 'I find many people don't take the time to do this. Now, who's email is sitting in my email box, and probably doesn't get deleted.

When following up, keep that person in mind. Let them know it was a pleasure to meet them. Let them know that you would like to learn more about them. You would like to know how to refer business to them.

Ask them how the business mixer worked out for them. Who did they meet that would be a good referral source. Invite them out for coffee. Get to know them.

If you want to build an impromptu referral meeting, invite a friend or associate that may be a good lead source for them.

Follow up, follow up, follow up. Remember, Follow Up.

Joining a Structured Networking Group

Let's consider various networking groups. What it takes to join, how do we decide on which one will be best.

Many people ask me which groups are the best, the biggest. Where can I do the most business?

I don't particularly know for sure. But you will. As I mentioned earlier navigate through different internet sites like Google and Meet Up to discover which structured groups are available to you.

Some of the most well-known structured organizations are LeTip International, and BNI. They both have chapters that meet weekly. The reason they meet weekly is because if you see each other week after week, month after month, you'll probably be on each other's mind continuously. How can I forget about you? As soon as a client, or a friend, mentions a problem, a need or a want, I quickly remember someone from my family of friends that I can recommend. You become the go to person. Your clients will depend on you as well. They know they can call you, and you'll recommend someone to fill their need, whether it's their need, or a client, family or friend.

These organizations have By-Laws that are required to be followed. Many business people, like the accountability, and some do not. We know being in business takes discipline and accountability, and many business owners choose resources like these because they work.

When looking for a structured networking group, no matter what it is called, look carefully at the members. Just because a group may have a lot of members, doesn't mean you'll get tons of business. You might, and you might not.

Look at the business categories associated with the group. These can be considered Strong Referral Sources or Power Partners as one organization refers to them.

For example; if you're a Financial Advisor, some of your closest referral sources may be the CPA, Banker, Wills Trusts, & Estates Attorney. Does the group your considering have these businesses represented?

If you're a Plumbing Contracting, who is the Realtor, Property Manager, Pool Service that you can network closely with? Now it doesn't mean you won't get business from the others outside of your immediate sphere of influence, you will. But you may want to make sure these individuals are represented.

Interview as many of the members as you can before you join. Not only will you learn how they can refer to you, but you'll also learn who they network with and how you can help them.

Find out how many business leads change hands in the chapter. Ask what the last representative in your business, did in transactions as a member.

Check out the leadership. Most of the structured, organized groups announce committee reports during their meeting. Notice how professionally done their committee reports are. Are they competent in their responsibility, and serious about their commitment to the members?

Are they too serious, or do they bring enjoyment to the meeting? Sometimes Board Members are too engrossed with keeping to the program that they don't enjoy being there. If that's the case, say thanks for having me and look elsewhere.

I was a Membership Chair for many years in my own networking chapter, and I remember one morning warmly greeting one of our members, shouting a vibrant Good Morning, asking "how are you today"?

His answer to me was "I'm here aren't I". I thought to myself, why is this guy here. Maybe we should replace him with someone that wants to be here.

When you walk into the room, notice the dynamics and energy. Are the members smiling and friendly? Are they happy to see each other? Are they shaking hands. Hugging, laughing together? You can tell if they enjoy being with each other.

Were you greeted warmly when you walked in. Did anyone explain the agenda, and introduce you around?

Most structured, professional and successful networking groups have a cost to membership. Maybe about a $1,000 a year. That's only $83.34 per month. Heck, you're probably going to spend that much monthly on breakfast or lunch anyway.

If a group meets in the morning, you're probably getting something to eat as well.

I've heard some people complain about paying to be in a networking group. I feel where there's a cost, there is value. Don't hesitate to ask what the cost covers.

Successful groups have a voting process, they don't allow in just anyone.

Bottom line is, how did you feel about everyone?

Becoming successful in a Structured Leads Organization.

Let's look at becoming successful in a Structured Professional leads chapter.

First couple of meetings you're getting to know everyone. Here are Ten Items that can help you become a successful networker in your structured meeting environment.

1) Try to meet at least two to three of the members individually each week. Now if you're a group of twenty or more this could take some time to meet everyone, but don't worry about that. Your main purpose here is to get to know them.
Set a business appointment with each one letting them know you want to find out how to send clients there way. Don't leave it up to memory, take notes when you meet with them. Believe me, they will be impressed that you care enough to write down key information they share with you.

At this point you want to get to know more about them than they know about you. Be truly interested in learning about them. Ask for a tour if they have a shop, such a print shop or large office environment.

Ask each member you meet individually with, what they know about you and your business. get a feeling of what they think of you.

This will take time and effort, but imagine if you met with each member, and each member gave you a worthwhile business deal. Now it's time well spent. You never know what business is waiting for you if you don't show up.

2) When you give your "commercial" each meeting, remember to practice it prior to, and make it count. Ask members what they would like to hear from you. Don't take it upon yourself to know what they want to hear. You might be surprised what they would like.

3) Listen to everyone's commercial as they give them. Take one thing from each commercial and decide what you liked best about it.

4) Be early for every meeting. This is the time to get to know each other. Consider your networking meeting, a scheduled business appointment. How many times do you show up after, your client gets to the

appointment. You're usually early when a client expects you. These are your client appointments each week so be there early.

5) Get involved. Don't just attend the meeting. Take on a job responsibility. The more you're involved the more you get noticed. The more you get noticed, the more you're thought of during the week. And that brings more business.

6) Help bring in new members. Nothing better than bringing in the people you're already networking with. When you're out at networking events, invite them to your leads group. Remember these are people already familiar with networking and sharing contacts. Everyone you bring into your group, becomes your loyal referral source.

7) Set the example for others. If you set the bar, others will follow.

8) Be accountable and honest with each member. Remember you will be sitting across the table from them every week.

9) When guests visit a meeting, always call them the next day and follow up. Ask how they liked it. What did they think? Who did they see that would be a good referral source for them? I have coached many people

to do this. The ones that practice it, make more referrals than they imagined. And all it takes is a phone call. Not an email or text. You can't open up a dynamic conversation in an email. When you converse personally, you share information and personality that you normally wouldn't in an email. I used to call every guest that attended my networking group. I wanted to know what they liked about it. I wanted to know if they would come back to the next meeting, so I could learn more about them and figure out how to send them clients. Nothing about me, it was all about them. I received more business from guests than I ever thought possible because I made the effort to see what they thought about our meeting. What I heard many times on the other end of that phone, was them asking me a question about my business, and many times if I could help them or a friend of theirs. All because I made the effort to contact them.

10) When you know a certain business owner your networking chapter could use as a new member, invite them. If you're using someone you like and feel confident in referring, bring them into your fold. Why not have people you already use. If you have a certain type of business that would be helpful to you or your membership but don't know anyone in that industry, pick some contacts out of your phone and ask them for a reference. It's a warm call. You're calling

someone you feel comfortable with asking for a recommendation.

When they pass along the recommendation, and you call, it's another warm call. Someone referred you. Just like when someone refers you to a restaurant they like, you don't feel awkward going there. You can use that same thought when looking for someone to introduce to your business leads group.

With all the work there is to networking, you probably didn't realize how systematic it could be. It's up to you, to put in the time if you want. What I will reiterate, is that relationships take time to build, just like your business. Just because you get licensed in a field of expertise, doesn't mean you'll be a success; your success is up to you.

It's time and efforts that produce the fruits of your labor.

Conclusion

Networking is only one letter different than Notworking. Like any other arm of your marketing campaign, you put forth your time and best effort to make it as productive as possible.

I have formed many relationships with many people over the years from networking. The personal and business connections have opened many doors along the way. Many of the relationships have molded me into the individual I am today.

From meeting and greeting the variety of individuals I have over time, I have learned how different, and similar many of us are.

Many people have taught me ways, in which to communicate successfully and many have educated me on how relationships materialize from strategic and chance meetings.

When I facilitate my seminars and workshops, I may sound like I am the expert in what to do and how to do it, but I see it as a learning experience. Every time I get up to speak to an audience, I am taking back information for myself in learning new ways to educate others.

My audience inspires my ideas. If they didn't give me the chance to address them, I would not learn the tips in expressing myself to help them.

From when I first arrived in Las Vegas I knew that to grow a business and fit into the community, I had to meet and relate to as many business owners as possible.

I first started an Office Janitorial Business.

I went to the local chamber picking up as many brochures and business cards as I could. Thumbing through every one of them to familiarize myself with who had the footing in the local community.

I walked door to door canvassing the city, soliciting for business. Meeting new people every day. It wasn't long after, that I started running into people I had approached weeks before.

That's when I realized I needed to make my claim in the community and get others to recognize the fact that I was around to stay, and not going anywhere.

Soon after, I began attending a philanthropic organization helping youngsters with disabilities.

Although this was a good networking opportunity it didn't have the business model I needed at the time to increase my business, but it did offer some degree of, not only personal satisfaction, but a lead into the business community.

I attended a Chamber of Commerce business mixer in March of that year. While mixing around, a gentleman introduced himself to me and explained to me he was starting a new business leads group called LeTip. He introduced himself as Pete Shevlin, an Insurance guy who is spearheading an upcoming leads group. I didn't know it at the time, but this chance meeting, was a turning point in my life. Pete introduced me to the world of structured networking. An organization with the sole purpose of "face to face" business referrals. A serious club for networking.

Pete Shevlin changed my life that day. He also became one of my dearest friends until the day he passed away.

Little did I know that this was the start of a lifelong friendship.

This was also the start of my internship in the decades of how I would be received and receive others in the world of building business relationships.

Where will you be networking? Who will you meet that may become your newest lifelong business relationship?

What stories will you tell of the grand opportunities you have experienced in your networking journey?

I want to know.

About the Author

John D'Acunto has been involved with structured business networking since 1993. His experiences in various businesses and sales helped countless business professionals navigate through the world of building and sustaining strong business relationships through the art of networking.

His passion for helping others connect, came from early childhood. When John's parents divorced, he felt out of place engaging in group conversation, and had to force himself to feel part of the crowd.

With that feeling of detachment, arose a desire to strengthen his need for engagement and focus his energies on how to participate in conversation.

John explains, "I always felt valuable listening and coaching on business related issues and challenges, to help others learn new techniques on building business relationships".

John is a seasoned Public Speaker and Certified Professional Coach mastering in the techniques of Networking, Leadership Skills, and the unique approach of Energy Leadership.

Over the years he has succeeded in starting and operating his own janitorial business, managing a sales team for Nevada's largest payroll company at the time, and going on to a career in the mortgage business. His experience of working in different businesses has given him a unique sense of how to help others learn to build their relationships for personal and business growth. Although John's passion is helping business professionals succeed, he also enjoys Sailing on any body of water that's wet, motorcycling, hiking, while spending time with his family.

Made in the USA
Las Vegas, NV
15 April 2021